Sunshine

Activity Book 4

Erarbeitet von
Stefanie Aschkar (Konstanz)
Tanja Beattie (Ebersberg)
Nadine Kerler (Ulm)
Caroline Schröder (München)
Maria Skejic (Frankfurt am Main)

Auf der Grundlage der Ausgabe von
Birgit Hollbrügge
und Ulrike Kraaz

Deine **interaktiven Gratis-Übungen** findest du hier:

1. Gehe auf scook.de.
2. Gib den unten stehenden Zugangscode in die Box ein.
3. Hab viel Spaß mit deinen Gratis-Übungen.

Dein Zugangscode auf
www.scook.de | 9329c-q6vwa

Cornelsen

Contents

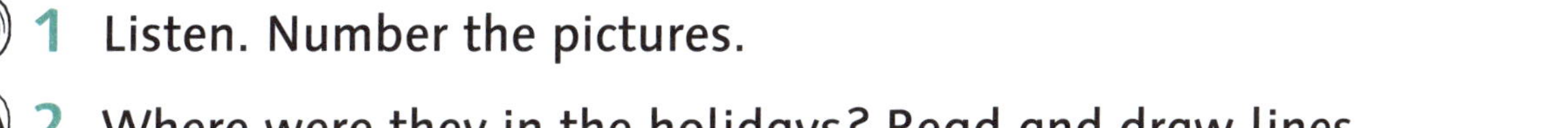

1 Listen. Number the pictures.

2 Where were they in the holidays? Read and draw lines.

☐ ☐ ☐ ☐

holidays in London

holidays in Rome

holidays in Ankara

holidays at home

3 Read the chant.

I was in London.
She was in Rome.
He was in Ankara.
And where were you?

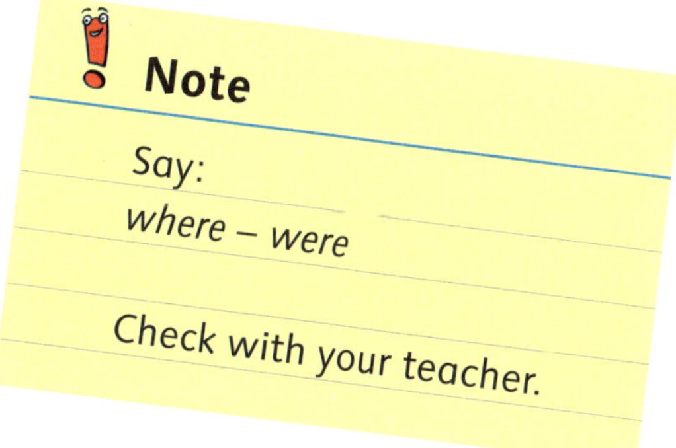

Note

Say:
where – were

Check with your teacher.

4 Talk about the holidays. Ask: *Where were you in the holidays?*

5 Write your own chant. Draw.

I was in ________________

__________ was in __________

____

____

____

Note

Wochentage werden im Englischen groß geschrieben!

1 Number the days in the right order.

2 Two days are on the weekend. Circle the words.

Talk to a partner. Say: *Monday is number …*

☐ Wednesday ☐ Saturday ☐ Tuesday ☐ Thursday

☐ Friday ☐ Monday ☐ Sunday

3 Complete the sentence.

________________ and ________________
are on the weekend.

4 Complete the sentences.

see you · sorry · time

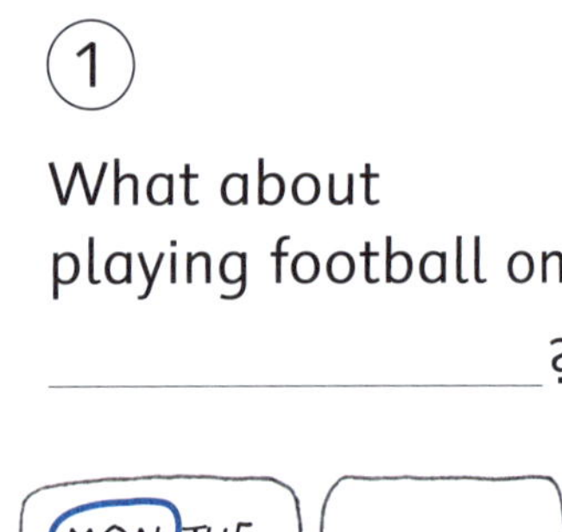

(1) What about playing football on ______________?

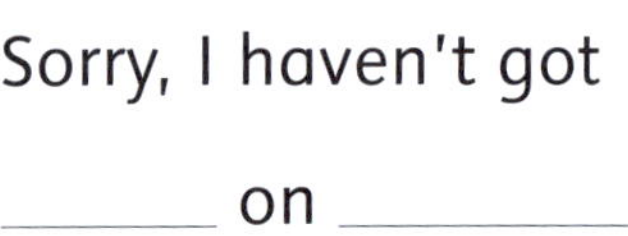

Sorry, I haven't got ______ on ________

(2) What about watching TV on ______________?

OK. ______________
on ______________

(3) What about meeting friends on ______________?

________ I haven't got time on ____________

1 Listen. Number the pictures.

blue · green · grey · red

2 Read. Complete the sentences. Check with a partner.

Harry is on the ________ bus. The train to London is ________

Kate's dad has got a ________ car. The underground is ________

Note

one bus – two bus**es**
one train – two train**s**

3 What is missing? Write or draw.

Make up your own row. Check with a partner.

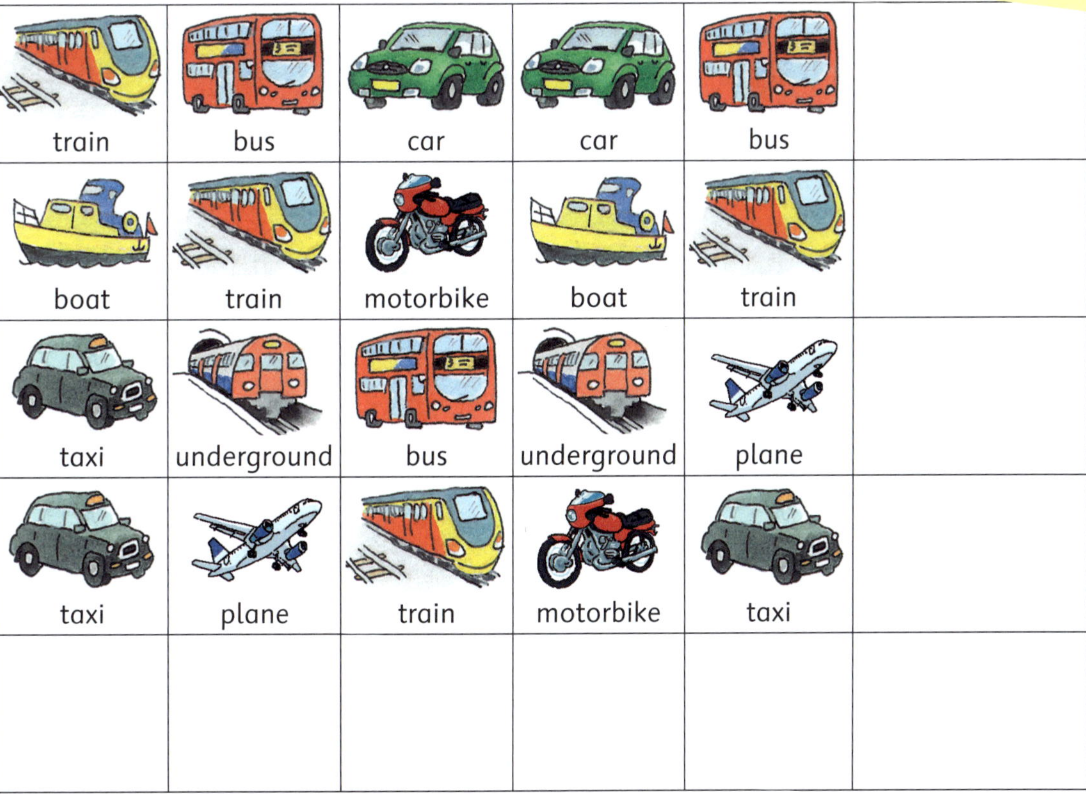

train	bus	car	car	bus	
boat	train	motorbike	boat	train	
taxi	underground	bus	underground	plane	
taxi	plane	train	motorbike	taxi	

16 **1 Listen. Write the missing words.**

bus · boat · car · taxi · underground

1. Harry, Kate and her dad go to Tower Bridge by  ______
2. They go to the London Zoo by ______
3. ______ go to Buckingham Palace by  ______
4. ______ to Big Ben by  ______
5. ______ the London Eye by  ______

2 Number the sights.

What day do they go to London Zoo, ...? Talk to a partner.

3 Find the words.

4 Write the missing letters.

R	F	T	1	O	N	D	2	N		E	Y	E	Z	T	B	U	S	O	P
A	C	P	B	U	C	K	I	3	G	H	A	M		P	A	L	A	C	E
G	D	L	O	N	4	O	N		Z	5	O	V	R	T	A	X	I	W	R
U	N	D	E	R	G	R	O	U	N	D	B	B	I	G		B	E	6	W
C	B	O	A	T	R	R	I	V	E	R		T	H	A	M	E	S	V	E
T	W	N	H	S	R	C	M	L	O	T	R	A	I	N	W	T	S	I	O

Solution:

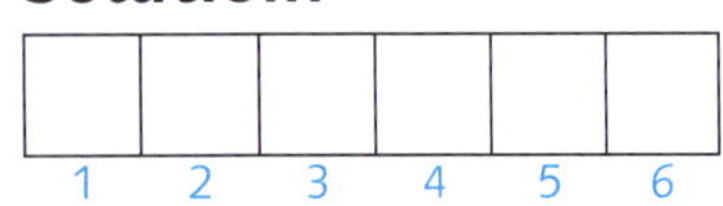

1	2	3	4	5	6

1 What time is it? Complete the sentences.

eight · eleven · five · four · nine · one · seven · six · ten · three · twelve · two

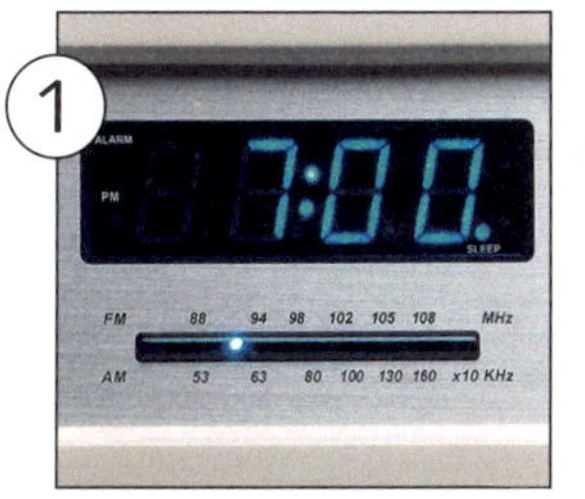

← It's ____________ o'clock.

It's __________ o'clock. →

← It's ____________ o'clock.

______________________ →

← ______________________

______________________ →

2 Plan your day in London. Write down sights and times.

3 Talk about your plan. Say: *At nine o'clock, I want to go to ...*

 1 Look at the boat tickets. Read the speech bubbles.

  2 Fill in the prices and the times. Check with a partner.

bus	all sights	£ 1.50	10:45
underground	all sights	£ 1.50	09:30
boat	London Eye	£	
	Tower Bridge	£	
	Big Ben	£	

Let's go to the London Eye by boat.

How much is it?

It's £1.20.

When is the next boat?

It's at 12:15.

Waterloo to Tower Bridge
on TUE 26 MAY
Fare: Single (Child) £1.20
L1238/00167 (08:15)
Retain Ticket for Inspection

Waterloo to Big Ben
on SUN 24 MAY
Fare: Single (Child) £3.60
L1238/00167 (11:30)
Retain Ticket for Inspection

Tower Bridge to London Eye
on THU 28 MAY
Fare: Single (Child) £1.20
L1238/00167 (12:15)
Retain Ticket for Inspection
Not Transferable

 19 3 Listen. What would they like to eat?

 4 Read the text. Write the missing words.

 Make up your own dialogue.

Harry: A __________ and __________ sandwich, please.
Man: White or brown __________?
Harry: Brown, please. And __________.
Man: Sorry, we don't have chips.
That's £2.60, please.
Harry: Thank you.

bread · cheese · chicken · chips · egg · ham · salad · water

Kate: A __________ sandwich, please.
Man: With or without salad?
Kate: With __________, please. But no __________. And some __________, please.
Man: Here you are. That's £3, please.
Kate: Thank you.
Man: You're welcome.

1 Write a postcard.

 Read the text. Write a text message.

Note

SMS language

How RU? = How are you?
Gr8 = great
KL = cool
Lk = like
Lndn = London
CU = see you

Ich fand die Aufgabe: leicht mittel schwer

1 What time is it?

_______________ (Name) und ich haben uns gegenseitig gefragt, wie spät es ist. ☐

Diese Zeiten haben wir uns diktiert:

2 Let's go to Big Ben.

Ich habe mit _______________ (Name) das Gespräch geführt. ☐

Wir haben dazu diese Minibildkarten benutzt:

Let's go to:

Let's go by:

3 Ich habe diese Wörter für *food* geschrieben. ☐

Das möchte ich noch besser können:

26 **1** Listen. Number the pictures.

2 Match the words to the pictures. Write the words.

☆ Which two weather words have no picture? Check with your partner.

bike · bus · car · ice cream · jacket · ~~park~~ · shoes · taxi

cloudy · foggy · rainy · snowy · sunny · windy

park

3 Draw the weather. Write.

☆ Write two more sentences. Talk to a partner.

What's the weather like on …?

Wednesday

Thursday

Friday

Sunday

Tuesday

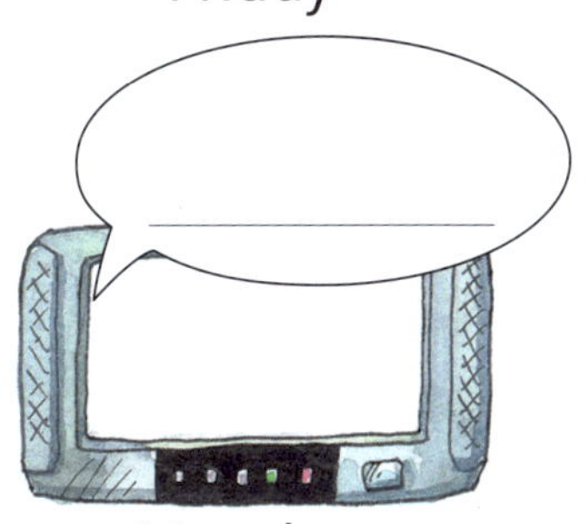
Monday

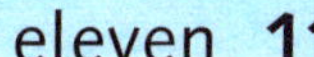

1 Read the temperatures.

2 Write the temperatures. Play Bingo.

3 Talk to a partner. Ask: *What temperature is it today?*

☆ Play again.

	Monday	Tuesday	Wednesday	Thursday	Friday	Saturday	Sunday
Game 1							
Game 2							

4 Read the sentences.

5 Listen and number. Circle the missing sentences.

- ☐ Today is Wednesday.
- ☐ Have a nice day.
- ☐ I'm Ted Miller.
- ☐ Here's the weather.
- ☐ Good morning.
- ☐ Today is Thursday.
- ☐ It's sunny today.
- ☐ It's 18°.
- ☐ Goodbye.
- ☐ This is BBC 1.
- ☐ It's rainy and cloudy today.

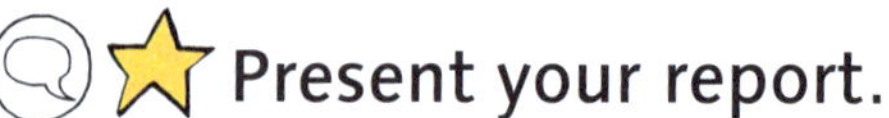

6 Write your own weather report with a partner.

7 Read your report.

☆ Present your report.

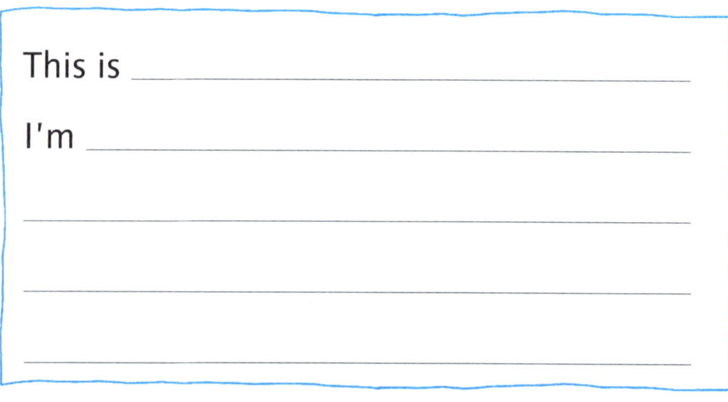

This is ____________________

I'm ____________________

____

____

____

Note

thirteen = 13
three = 3
fifteen = 15
five = 5

1 Read the words. Choose words for your rhyme.

☆ Find more words. Check with a partner. Use a dictionary.

spring	summer	autumn	winter
Easter bunny	swimming	wind	snow
daffodils	sunshine	pumpkin	reindeer
rain	ice cream	apples	pullover
______	______	______	______

2 Write a rhyme.

3 Present it in class.

____

______________________________ in spring.

____

What will ______________________ bring?

1 Write the months and seasons.

Find more words for the seasons.

autumn · spring · summer · winter

January · February · March · April · May · June · July · August · September · October · November · December

1 When is your birthday? Write the month and the date.

MON	TUE	WED	THU	FRI	SAT	SUN

2 Complete the sentences.

My name is ______________________

My birthday is in ______________________ (month)

______________________ (month) is in ______________________ (season)

The weather in ______________________ (month) is ______________________ (weather)

This year my birthday is on ______________________ (day)

3 What is typical for your birthday month? Draw or stick in a picture.

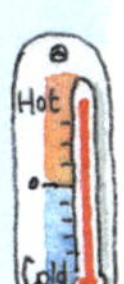

Ich fand die Aufgabe: leicht mittel schwer

1 Chant: Snowdrops in winter

Ich habe ______________ (Name) den *chant* *Snowdrops in winter* vorgelesen. ☐ ○ ○ ○

in winter. *in spring.* *in summer.*
What will autumn bring?

Ich habe den *chant* auswendig gesagt.

2 What's the weather like on …?

Monday	Tuesday	Wednesday	Thursday	Friday	Saturday	Sunday

______________ (Name) und ich haben uns gegenseitig das Wetter an verschiedenen Wochentagen diktiert. ☐ ○ ○ ○

3 A weather report

______________ (Name) und ich haben uns gegenseitig einen Wetterbericht vorgetragen. ☐ ○ ○ ○

☐ Monday ☐ Tuesday ☐ Wednesday ☐ Thursday
☐ Friday ☐ Saturday ☐ Sunday
☐ cloudy ☐ sunny ☐ windy ☐ snowy
☐ foggy ☐ rainy ☐ the temperature: ______________

Das möchte ich noch besser können:

____

1 Listen to the song.

2 Number the pictures.

3 What animal is not in the song? Circle the picture.

4 Complete the text.

Sing the song with a partner.

~~camel~~ · crocodile · elephant · hippo · lion · monkey · parrot · snake

1. The ____________ is the king of the jungle.
2. The ____________ is big and strong.
3. The ____________ is very dangerous.
4. The ____________ is very long.
5. The ____________ likes to swing through the branches.
6. The camel ____________ likes to walk, walk, walk.
7. The ____________ likes to sit in the mud all day.
8. The ____________ likes to talk, talk, talk, talk, talk, talk, talk, talk, talk, talk, talk.

 1 Find the words and circle them.

2 Write the words. (Two animals have no picture.)

☆ Find two more animals and draw.

ucrocodilelmelephantpihipporelioncwhalefmonkeydparrotlpsnakeup

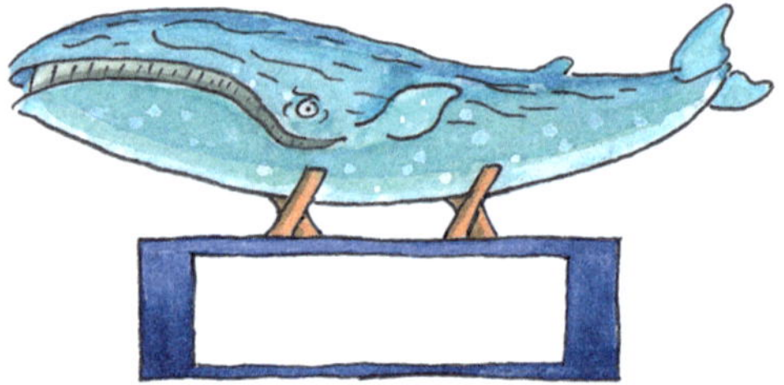

 3 How many animals are there? Write the numbers.

crocodiles · dinosaurs · elephants · hippos · lions · monkeys · parrots · snakes · whales

33 **1** Listen. Complete the sentences. What animals are missing?

☆ Make up two more dialogues. Work with a partner.

1 Excuse me, please. Where are the ____________?
They're upstairs, in room 31.

2 Excuse me, please. Where are the ____________?
They're downstairs, in room 15.

3 Excuse me, please. Where are the lions?
They're ____________ in room ____

4 ____________ ____________ ____________?
They're ____________ in room ____

34 **2** Listen. What animal is it? Fill in the name.

3 Number the sentences in the right order.

☆ Write the rhyme.

- [ ] The ____________ goes
- [ ] He's terribly big
- [ ] And goodness gracious,
- [ ] And he's terribly fat.
- [ ] Like this, like that.
- [ ] He has big toes,
- [ ] What a nose!
- [ ] He has no fingers,

1 Listen to your partner. Name the animals and the body parts.

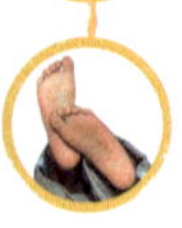

2 Write the words.

an elephant's · a crocodile's · a dinosaur's · a lion's · a monkey's · a parrot's

arm · ear · feet · leg · nose · tail · teeth

1 an elephant's leg

2 ______

3 ______

4 ______

5 ______

6 ______

7 ______

8 ______

9 ______

3 Where do the animals live? Tick (✓) or cross (✗).

Write more sentences. Draw pictures.

- [ ] Monkeys and snakes live in trees.
- [ ] Elephants and whales live in rivers.
- [ ] Parrots live in the jungle.
- [ ] Crocodiles live in the sea.
- [ ] Lions live in the bush.
- [ ] Hippos live in rivers.
- [ ] ______
- [ ] ______

Portfolio: **Animal presentation**

1 Glue or draw a picture of your animal.

2 Write about your animal.

3 Present your text.

I want to speak about

____

____

____

____

____

____

____

____

Make notes.

Know your text.

Speak loudly.

Look at the class.

Show pictures.

Ich fand die Aufgabe: leicht mittel schwer

1 Rhyme: The elephant

Ich habe den Reim auf der CD angehört. ☐

Ich habe ____________ (Name) den Reim vorgelesen. ☐

Ich habe den Reim auswendig aufgesagt. ☐

2 Where are the lions?

____________ (Name) und ich haben uns gegenseitig gefragt, wo die Tiere in unseren Museen ausgestellt sind. Wir haben die Tiernamen in die Räume geschrieben (Kopiervorlage 24, Aufgabe 2) und geprüft, ob wir sie richtig eingetragen haben. ☐

3 Talking about animals.

Ich habe ____________ (Name) meine Tier-Portfolioseite präsentiert (Seite 21). ☐

Ich habe mir den Vortrag von ____________ (Name) über ____________ angehört. ☐

Folgende Körperteile des Tieres wurden beschrieben:

arms ☐ ears ☐ feet ☐ legs ☐ nose ☐ teeth ☐

Das möchte ich noch besser können:

____

1 Listen. What club do they want to go to? Draw lines.

2 Write sentences.

Emily wants to go to the ______________________________

Kate ______________________________

fit kids club

judo club

pet club

computer club

dance club

girls' football club

Samir ______________________________

Harry ______________________________

3 What club do you want to go to? Talk to a partner.

4 Make a poster for the club.

1 Read the words.

2 Write the words. Check with a partner.

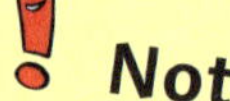

Note

one arm – two arm**s**
but:
one t**oo**th – two t**ee**th
one f**oo**t – two f**ee**t

arm
back
foot
hand
head
knee
leg
shoulder
toe
tummy

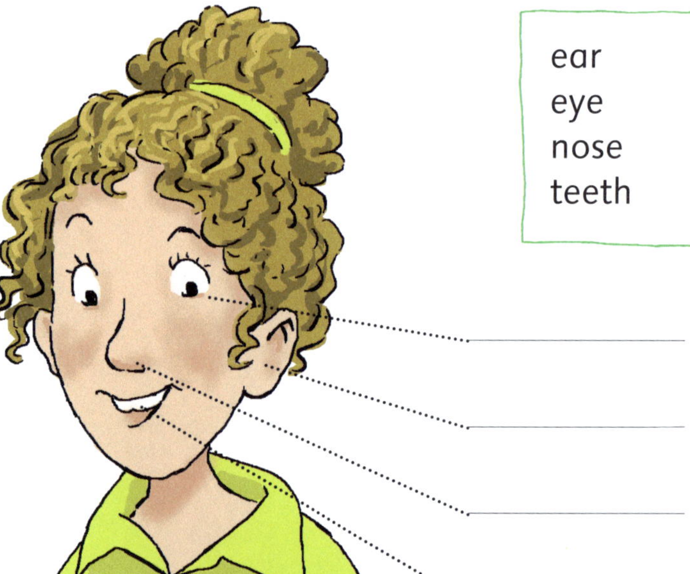

ear
eye
nose
teeth

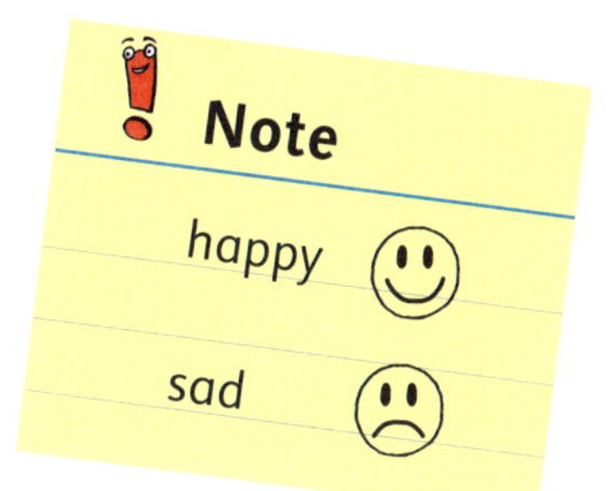

1 Read and number.

2 Listen to your partner. Guess the monster.

☆ Write a text about monster number 4.
Is the monster happy or sad?

1  2  3  4 

☐ The monster has got 1 head, 2 eyes, 1 nose, 1 mouth, 5 teeth, 4 ears, 4 arms, 4 hands, 4 legs and 4 feet.

☐ The monster has got 1 head, 2 round ears, 1 big eye, 2 noses, 1 mouth, no teeth, 2 long arms, 2 hands and 2 legs.

☐ The monster has got 1 head, 3 eyes, 1 nose, 1 mouth, 1 tooth, no ears, a fat tummy, 2 arms, 2 hands and 1 foot.

 3 Draw your own monster. Write about your monster.

This is my monster:

1 Listen and move.

bend · hop · put · stand · stretch · touch

2 Number the pictures. (Two pictures and words are wrong.)

3 Complete the sentences. Check with a partner. Present in class.

arms · hands · head · knee · leg · tummy

1. ____________ on one ____________
2. ____________ that ____________
3. ____________ your ____________
4. ____________ your ____________ in the air.
5. ____________ your ____________

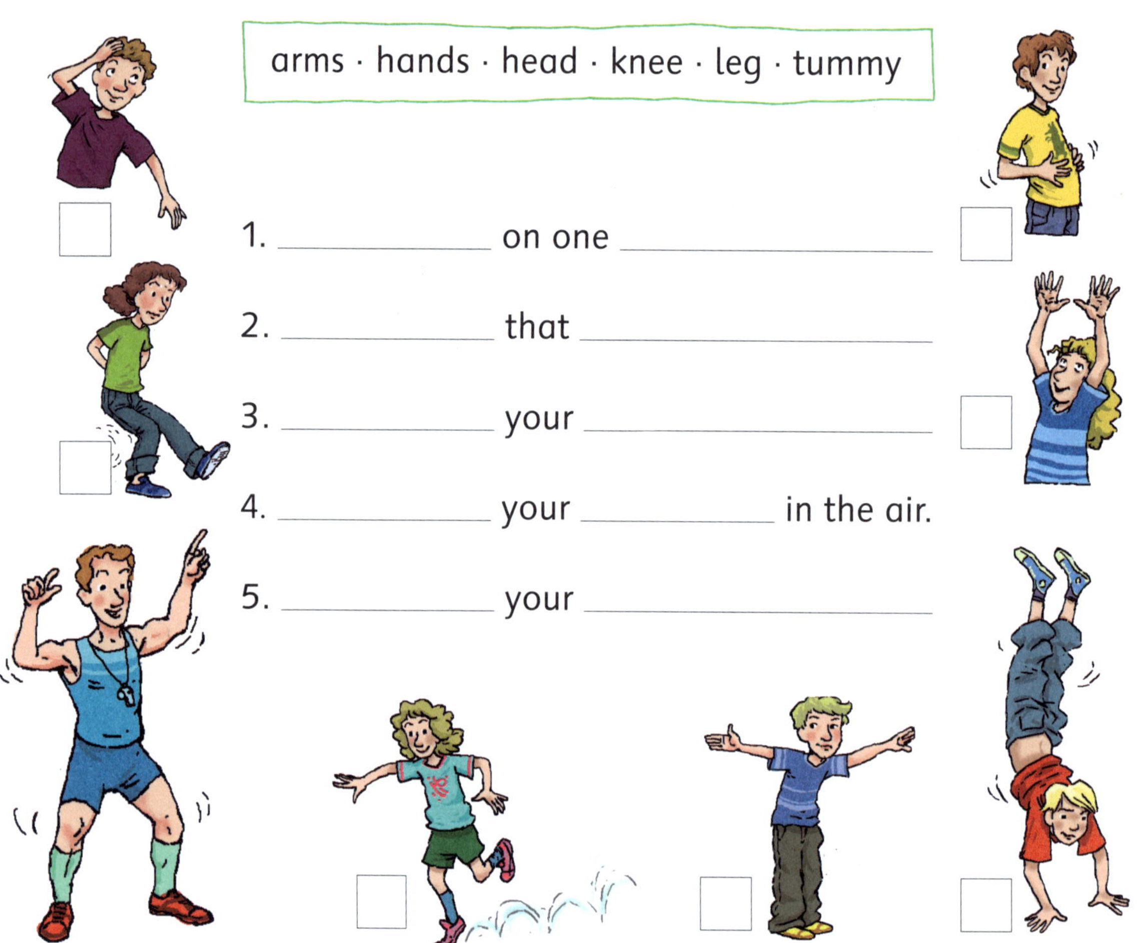

4 Make up a new fitness programme. Draw or write.

Do it with your group.

1 Complete the sentences. Check with a partner.

dance · do judo · play table tennis · ride a horse · ski · swim

1 

Kate can ______________

Emily can't

____

2 

3 

Samir ______________

Harry ______________

4 

2 What can the children in your class do? Write sentences.

______________ can ______________

______________ can ______________

____

Note

How many children can swim, ...?
Make a list.

3 How does the giraffe feel? Write.

It feels ______________

____

____

It feels ______________

____

____

1 Interview your partner. Complete the speech bubbles. (Look at page 23 and 30).

2 Talk to your partner.

☆ Present the dialogue.

A sports interview

Hi, can I ask you some questions about sport?

Yes, OK.

What's your favourite sport?

My favourite sport is ____________

What about ____________?
Can you play ____________ ____________?

No, I can't ____________.
But I can ____________ ____________

Do you go to the ____________ club on ____________?

No, I go to the ____________ on ____________?

Thanks for the interview. Bye!

You're welcome. Bye!

 **1** What sports can you do? What sports can't you do? Write.

I can ______________________________

____

I can't ______________________________

____

____

____

____

____

____

____

2 What sports are you good at? What sports don't you like?

 **3** Write about your family and friends. What are they good at?

They are good at ______________________________

____

Check your English

Ich fand die Aufgabe: leicht mittel schwer

1 Song: Reach for the sky

Ich habe mit der Klasse das Lied *Reach for the sky* gesungen. ☐

2 Fitness in the classroom

Ich habe ein eigenes Fitnessprogramm (Seite 26) erstellt und mit ______________ noch einmal ausprobiert. ☐

3 Can you ...?

______________ (Name) und ich haben uns gegenseitig befragt, welche Sportarten wir können. ☐

______________ (Name) can ______________

4 An interview

______________ (Name) und ich haben ein Interview zu sportlichen Aktivitäten geführt. ☐

☐ dance
☐ do judo
☐ play basketball
☐ play table tennis
☐ ride a horse
☐ run
☐ ski
☐ swim
☐ play football

Das möchte ich noch besser können:

____

Emails from the USA

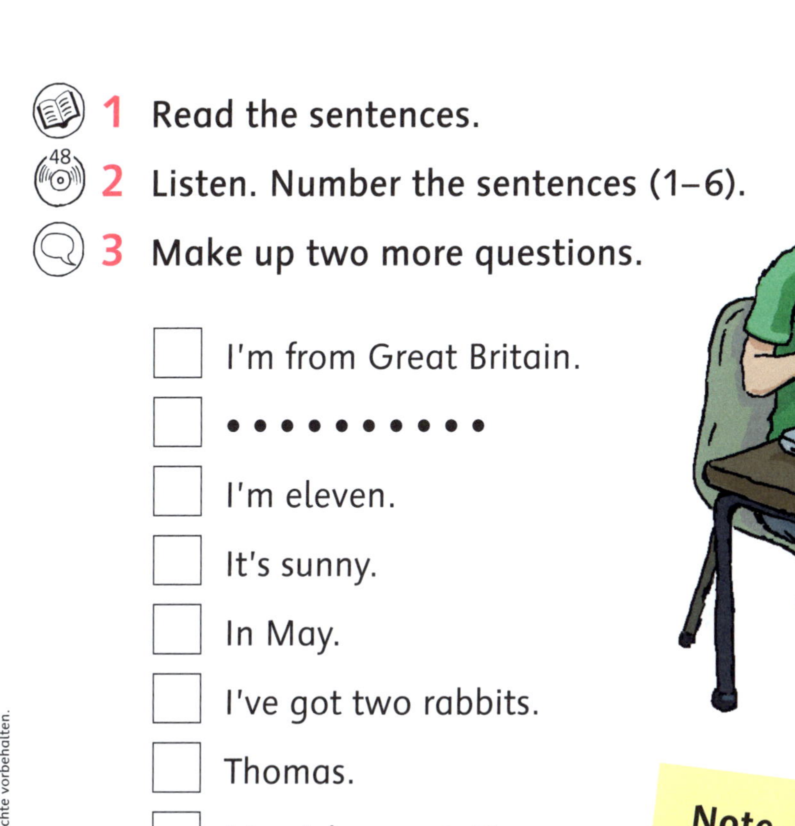

1 Read the sentences.

2 Listen. Number the sentences (1–6).

3 Make up two more questions.

- [ ] I'm from Great Britain.
- [ ] ••••••••••
- [ ] I'm eleven.
- [ ] It's sunny.
- [ ] In May.
- [ ] I've got two rabbits.
- [ ] Thomas.
- [ ] My nickname is Tom.

Note

Dein Name, deine Adresse, deine Telefonnummer oder dein Geburtsdatum gehen nicht jeden etwas an. Sprich immer zuerst mit deiner Lehrerin, deinem Lehrer oder deinen Eltern, bevor du im Internet von dir erzählst.

4 Write the answers.

Make up more questions. Interview your partner.

What's your name?	
How old are you?	
When's your birthday?	
Where are you from?	
What's your nickname?	

 **1** Read the text.

 **2** Write about yourself.

☆ Talk in class. Ask: *Where are you from? Where do you live? What's your address?*

Note

In den USA und in Großbritannien schreibst du die Hausnummer vor den Straßennamen:
50 King Street

And what about you?

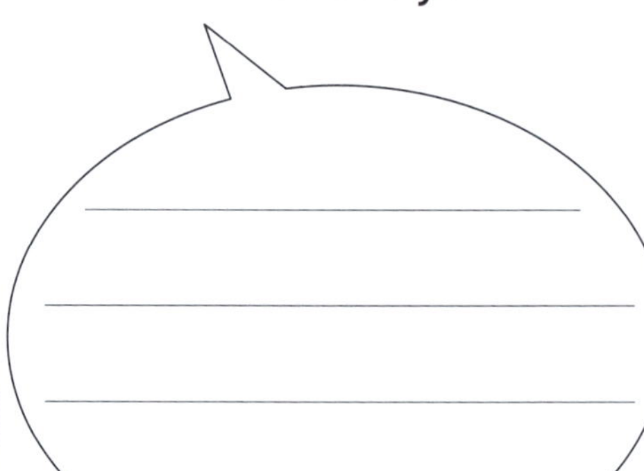

3 Read the sentences.

4 Write the family words.

My **father** is a mechanic.
My **grandmother** was a shop assistant.
My **sister** is a teacher.
My **grandfather** is a police officer.
My **brother** is a taxi driver.
My **mother** is a hairdresser.

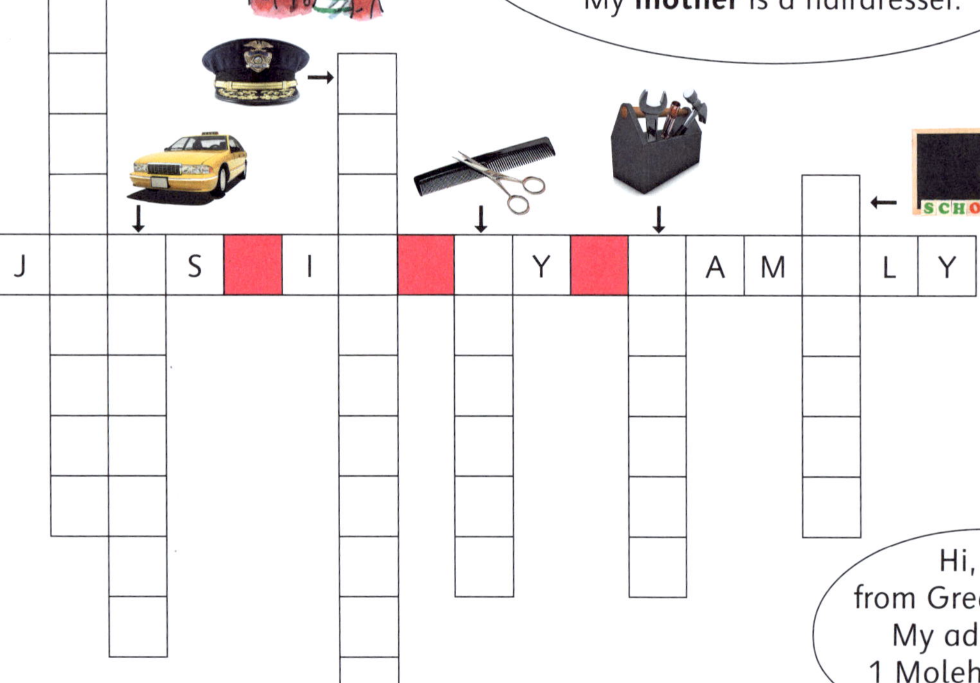

Hi, I'm from Great Britain. My address is 1 Molehill, Mole Town.

 **1 Read the words.**

 **2 Write the words.**

hairdresser · mechanic · police officer
shop assistant · taxi driver · teacher

She's a 

____

He's a 

____

She's a  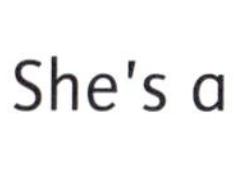

____

He's a 

____

She's a 

____

He's a 

____

 **3 Read the words and the text.**

 **4 Write the missing words in the email. Work with a partner.**

bus driver · dog · eleven · Germany · he · May ·
mother · playing with my friends · she · small house

Hi Michael,

I'm from ________________ and I'm ________________ years old.

My birthday is in ________. I live with my ________________ and two sisters. My mother's name is Sarah. ______ is a ________________.

We have got a ____________________ with a garden.

I've got a __________. His name is Rex. ______ is black and white.

My hobbies are ____ and writing emails. Please write and tell me about your family.

From,

Leon

1 Where does the bus stop? Listen and number.

Brooklyn Bridge
Central Park
Empire State Building
Statue of Liberty

2 Write down where the bus stops. Check with a partner.

1. The bus stops at ____________________. Let's have a picnic.
2. The bus stops at the ______________________________.
   Wow, what a big building!
3. The bus stops at a river. Over there is the ________________
   ____________________.
4. The bus stops at ______________________________.
   It's a very old bridge.

3 What does the police officer ask? Write down the answers.

★ Listen to your partner. Who is it? Find out.

Name: ________________________

City: ________________________

Street: ________________________

Phone number: __________________

Mother's name: __________________

Father's name: __________________

 1 Write an email to a friend.

 Send your email. Answer your friend's email.

My name is … · I'm … years old. · I've got a … ·
I'm from … · I live in … · My favourite lesson in school is … ·
My hobbies are … · My favourite sport is … ·
My mum / dad is a … · I like … · I don't like …

New message

To

Subject About me

Hi ____________________

Send

Ich fand die Aufgabe: leicht mittel schwer

1 Where do you live?

Ich habe ______ (Name) gesagt, wo ich wohne.

Ich habe nach seiner/ihrer Adresse gefragt. ☐

2 This is Matt's family

Matt

Ich habe Matts Familienmitglieder richtig aufgeschrieben.

Ich habe ______ (Name) gesagt, welche Berufe Matts Mutter, sein Vater und sein Bruder ausüben.

Ich habe gesagt, was meine Eltern beruflich machen. ☐

3 My email

Ich habe ______ (Name) meine E-Mail auf Seite 35 vorgelesen. ______ (Name) hat mir seine/ihre E-Mail vorgelesen. ☐

Das möchte ich noch besser können:

______

A school play

6

1 Look at the board. Write the words.

Is there a pupil in the classroom?

Yes, there is.

2 What's in the classroom? Ask your partner. Tick the words. (✓)

- [x] pupil
- [ ] ____________
- [ ] ____________
- [ ] ____________
- [ ] ____________
- [ ] ____________
- [ ] ____________
- [ ] ____________

3 Look at the dialogue. Fill in the missing words.

Pupil:	The ________ is coming.
Teacher:	Good morning, ________.
Pupil:	____________, Mrs Brown.
Teacher:	What ______ is it today?
Pupil:	It's ________ today.
Teacher:	Please write it on the ________.
	What's the ________ like?
Pupil:	It's ____________.
Teacher:	Where's Sally?
Pupil:	She's _____, Mrs Brown.

board · children · day · ill · Good morning · teacher · weather

Monday · Tuesday · Wednesday · Thursday · Friday

cloudy · cold · foggy · rainy · snowy · sunny · windy

4 Read the dialogue with your partner.

 1 Find the sentences to match the pictures.

 2 Colour the matching sentences red, blue or green.

 3 Number the red, blue and green sentences.

- [ ] She was in Rome.
- [ ] And goodness gracious, What a nose!
- [ ] Daffodils in spring.
- [ ] And where were you?
- [ ] Roses in summer.
- [1] The elephant goes Like this, like that
- [ ] Snowdrops in winter.
- [ ] I was in London.
- [ ] He has no fingers, He has big toes.
- [ ] He was in Ankara.
- [ ] What will autumn bring?
- [ ] I was at home.
- [ ] He's terribly big, And he's terribly fat.

4 Write down your favourite rhyme or chant.

5 Read it to your partner.

____

____

____

____

____

 **1** Read the words and sentences.

 64 **2** Listen and number the pictures.

 **3** Write the missing sentences.

 **4** Read with partners.

> Here's the London Eye. · Here's the River Thames. · I don't know the word. · That was bad. · This is Big Ben. · This is London Zoo. · This is Tower Bridge.

① Inspector: What do you know about London?

② Pupil 1: ______________________

③ Pupil 2: ______________________

④ Pupil 3: ______________________

⑤ Pupil 4: ______________________

⑥ Pupil 5: ______________________

… and this is … ______________________

⑦ Inspector: Buckingham Palace.

____

5 One word is wrong. Circle and write.

 Find headlines for the words.

river	(bike)	boat	bridge	bike
sister	teacher	pupil	school inspector	______
crocodile	lion	monkey	hamster	______
lunch box	pencil	ruler	rubber	______
winter	summer	May	spring	______
windy	sunny	rainy	happy	______
angry	late	happy	scared	______
Tuesday	March	January	June	______
scarf	trousers	oven	gloves	______

 **1** Find the words in the word puzzle.

 **2** Write the words next to the pictures.

G	U	I	N	E	A		P	I	G
P	E	N	M	S	T	R	A	I	N
H	A	R	R	Y	H	O	N	E	Y
F	O	O	T	B	A	L	L	I	S
B	I	K	E	T	H	E	R	A	T
S	C	H	O	O	L	T	A	X	I
	I	N	S	P	E	C	T	O	R

 **3** Find 6 more words. Write the words. Check with your partner.

 **4** Write sentences.

angry · good · happy · loud · sad · scared

1. The boy is

2. The girl is

3.

4.

5.

6.

Portfolio: **A school play**

1 The name of our school play was: ____________________

2 The play was on ____________________

3 This was our play:

Scene 1 ____________________

Scene 2 ____________________

Scene 3 ____________________

Scene 4 ____________________

Scene 5 ____________________

Scene 6 ____________________

Scene 7 ____________________

Scene 8 ____________________

4 I was a ____________________

5 My friend ____________ was a ____________

6 My favourite scene was ____________________

7 Draw a picture of your favourite scene or stick in a photo.

This is from scene ____________________

Check your English

Ich fand die Aufgabe: leicht mittel schwer

1 Rhyme

Ich habe ______________ (Name) den Reim ______________ vorgetragen (Seite 38). ☐

2 An invitation

Wir haben Einladungskarten zu unserer Aufführung geschrieben. ☐

3 The school inspector

Ich habe die Sprechblasen den 8 Szenen des Stückes *The school inspector* zugeordnet. ☐

Scene ______
I'm Mr McTidy.
Nice to meet you.

Scene ______
What do you know about London?
Here's the London Eye.

Scene ______
Do you speak German?
What's your name?

Scene ______
Have you got your books?
What about your pencil cases?

Scene ______
I'm Mr McTidy, the new caretaker.
Oh, no! Not the school inspector.

Scene ______
Sorry, I'm late.
Good morning, children.

Scene ______
I want to speak about crocodiles.
I'm scared of crocodiles!

Scene ______
Do you know a rhyme?
Of course we do.

Das möchte ich noch besser können:

____

71 **1** Listen. Write the words.

2 Say the words. Draw what's missing.

Write what's missing. Look in a dictionary.

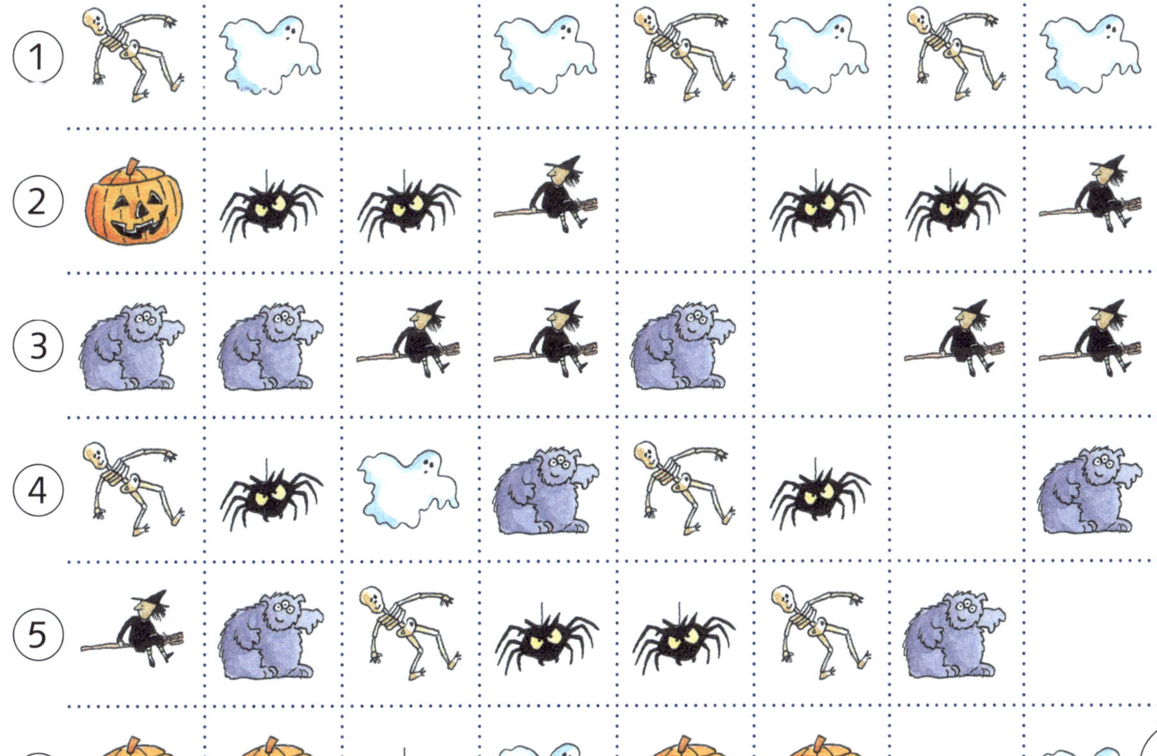

Special days: **Halloween**

1 Find 3 ghosts. Work with your partner.

Partner A   Partner B

2 Write what you can see here.

ghost · monster · pumpkin · skeleton · spider · witch

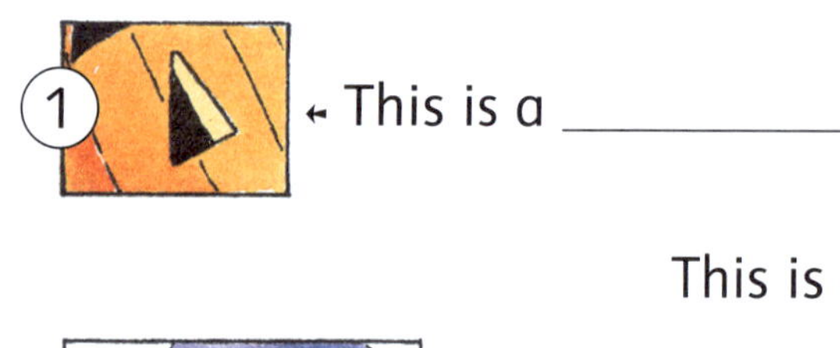
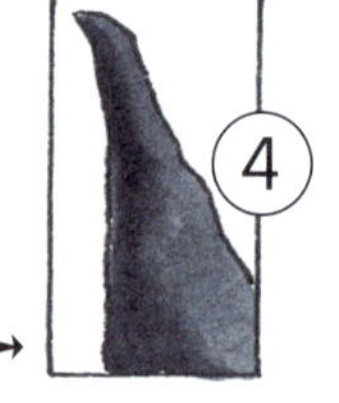

1 ← This is a ______________________

This is a ______________________ → 4

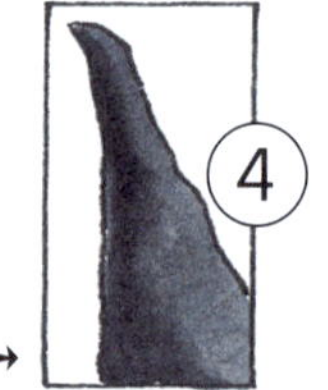

2 ← This is a ______________________

This is a ______________________ → 5

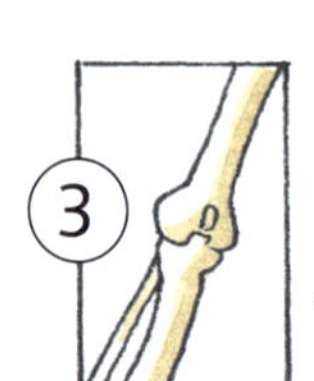
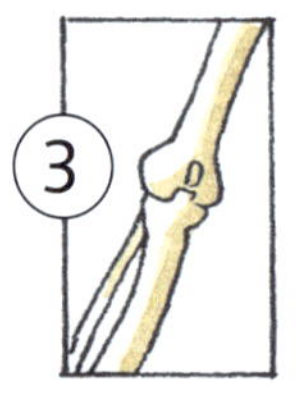

3 ← This is a ______________________

This is a ______________________ → 6

1 Talk about the pictures. Say: *Guy number one is wearing …*

74 **2** Listen. Number the children.

☆ Draw your own guy. Present your guy.

 **3** Play with a partner.

	A	B	C	D
1				
2				
3				
4				

London map A

	A	B	C	D
1				
2				
3				
4				

London map B

Special days: **Christmas**

 **1** Listen to the song.

 **2** Read the text.

 **3** Circle the right word.

 **4** Complete the text.

Rudolph the red-nosed ______________	reindeer · elephant
Had a very shiny ______________	mouth · nose
And if you ever saw it	
You would even say it ______________	glows · shines

All of the other reindeer	
Used to ______________ and call him names.	cry · laugh
They never let ______________ Rudolph	happy · poor
______________ any reindeer games.	play · join in

Then one ______________ Christmas Eve	foggy · sunny
______________ came to say:	Father Christmas · Santa
'Rudolph with your nose so ______________	bright · dark
Won't you guide my ______________ tonight?'	sleigh · plane

Then all the reindeer ______________ him	hated · loved
And they ______________ out with glee	whispered · shouted
'Rudolph the ______________ reindeer	green-nosed · red-nosed
You'll go down in history!'	

1 Listen. Point to the pictures.

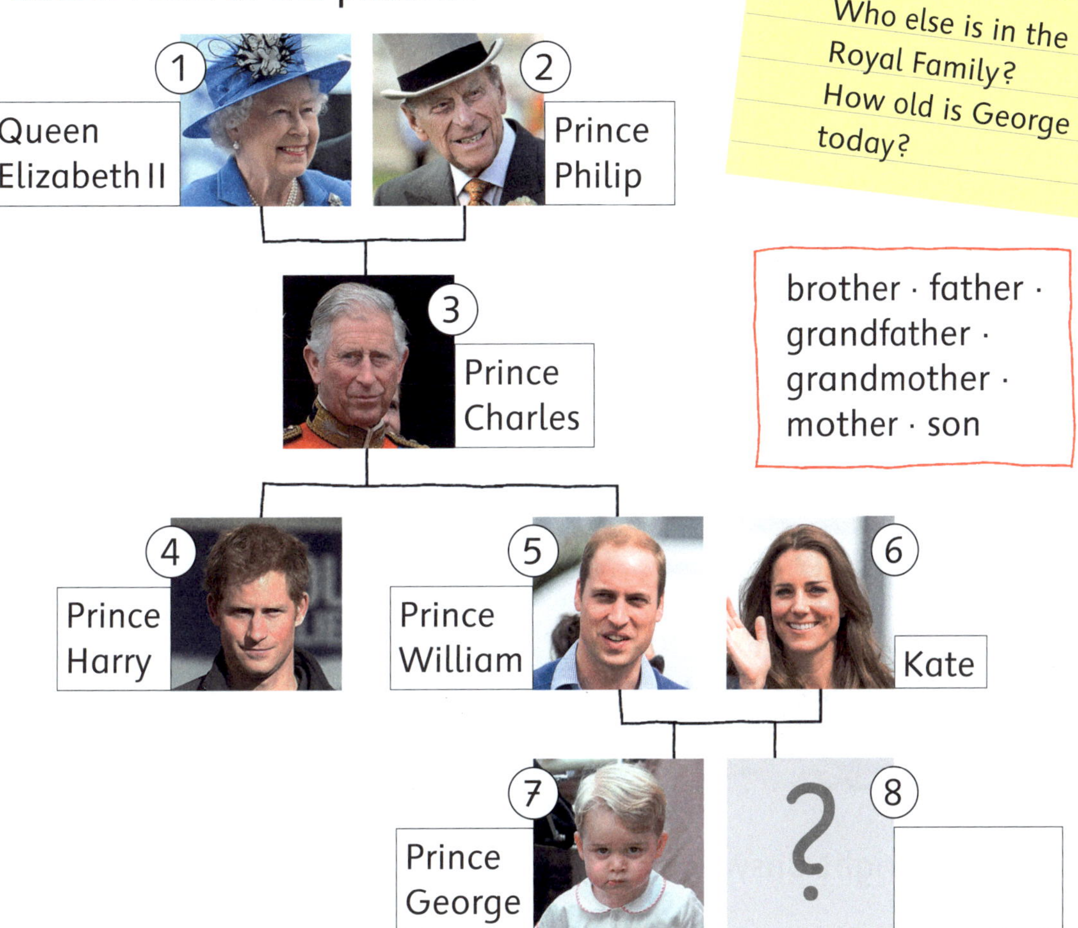

Note

Who else is in the Royal Family?
How old is George today?

brother · father · grandfather · grandmother · mother · son

2 Number the sentences. Write the words.

3 Write one more sentence.

- ☐ Queen Elizabeth is Prince Harry's ________________
- ☐ Prince Harry is Prince William's ________________
- ☐ Prince Philip is Prince Harry's ________________
- ☐ Kate is Prince George's ________________
- ☐ Prince Charles is Prince Harry's ________________
- ☐ Prince George is Kate's and William's ________________
- ☐ ________________

What about your own family? Talk to a partner.

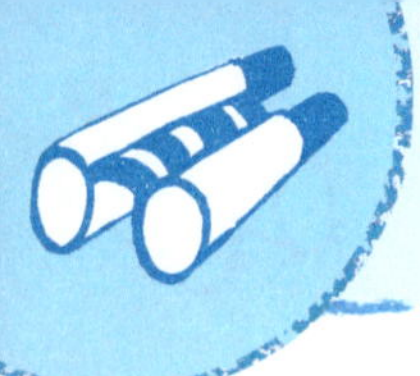

More to explore: Film **'On the beach'**

 **1** Find the right order. Number the pictures.

 **2** Tick the right answer. (✓)

 Write one more sentence. Work with a partner.

	right	wrong
Ben's dad says: 'I'm cold.'		
Ben helps Mr Mole out of the water.		
Mr Mole can fly.		
Mr Mole can't swim.		
The treasure is very small.		

 **3** Draw the treasure.

 Write.

It's a ___________________________

→ DVD 1

1 Complete the sentences.

Mr Mole: ______________________

What is that?

Mr Digger: It's an __________ bone.

They are at a ______________________

Goodness gracious!

What big ______________________!

It wasn't an ______________ bone.

And it wasn't a ______________ bone.

It was a ______________ bone.

animal · crocodile · dinosaur · elephant · feet · Goodness gracious! · museum

2 Draw the treasure.

Write.

It's a ______________________

→ DVD 3

1 Find the right order. Write the sentences. Number the pictures.

fun swimming is

found cross the I

toes your touch

can't we play cricket

2 Draw the treasure.

Write.

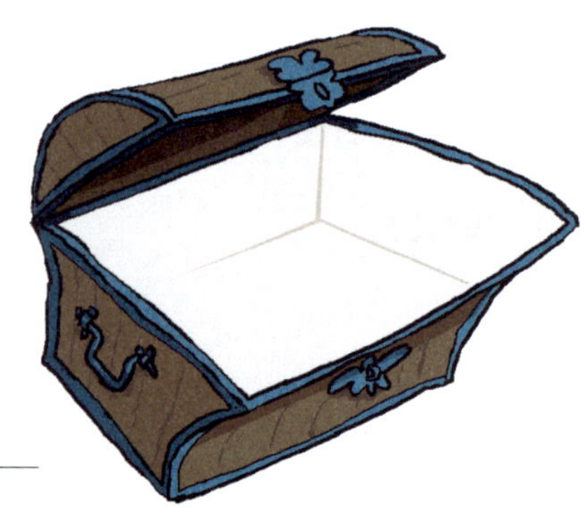

It's a ______________________

→ DVD 4

Word fields

Days of the week

Transport

Days of the week

My personal words

____

____

____

____

____

Transport

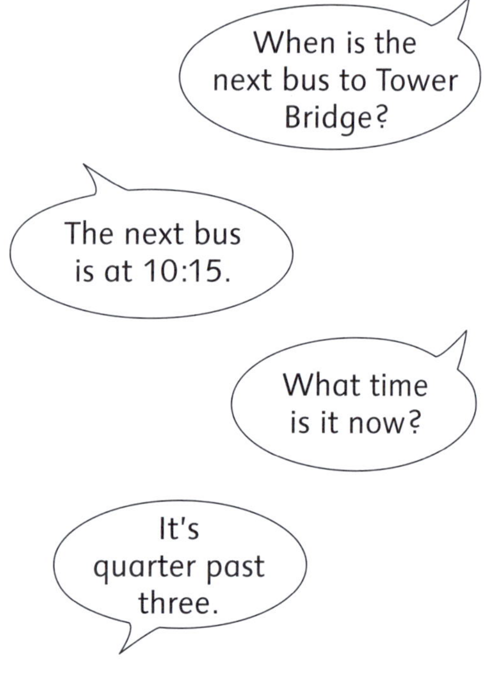

My personal words

____

____

____

____

____

Food

Weather and seasons

Food

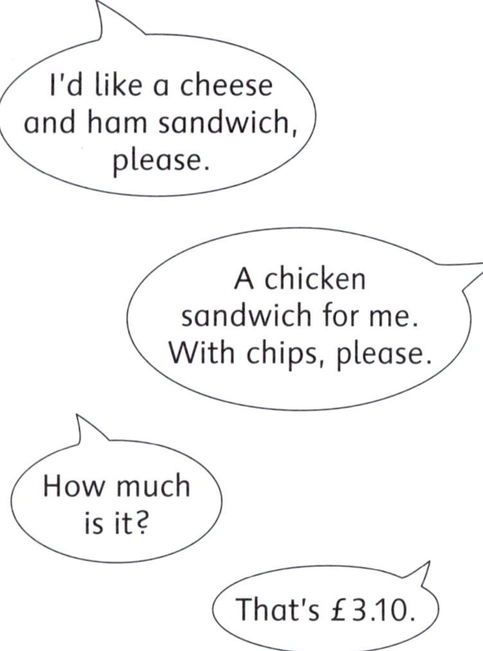

My personal words

____

____

____

____

____

Weather and seasons

My birthday is in summer.

What's the weather like in summer?

It's sunny and warm.

I was born in winter. It's snowy and cold in winter.

My personal words

____

____

____

____

____

Animals

Body parts

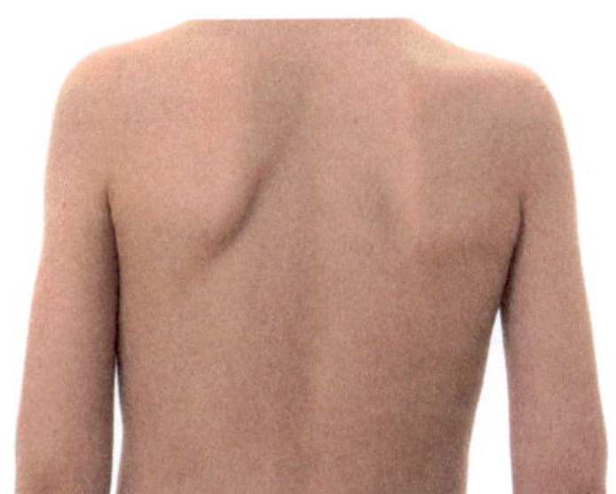
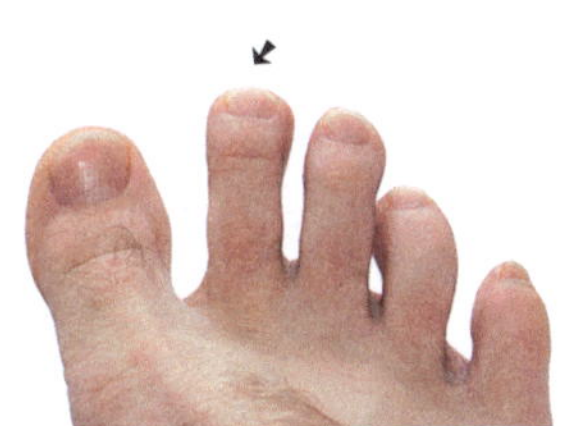

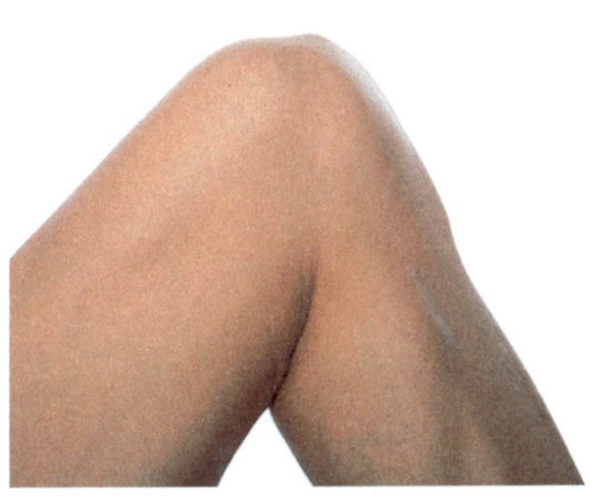
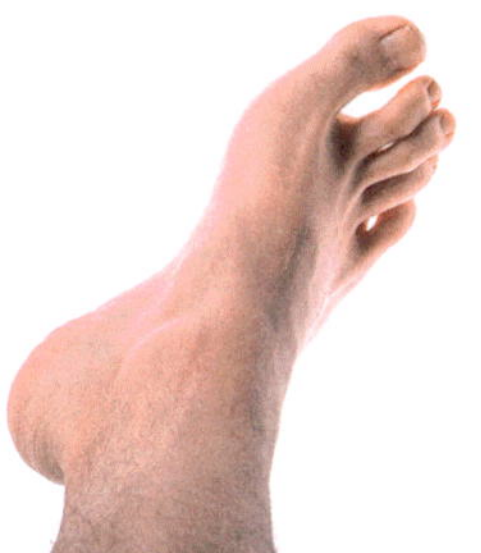
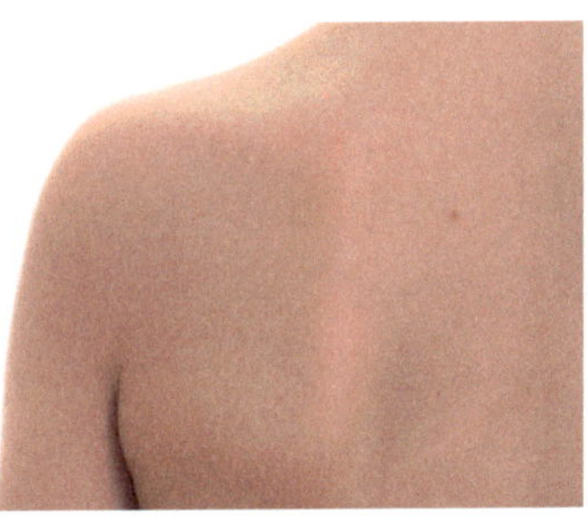

Animals

Excuse me, please. Where are the monkeys?

They are upstairs, in room number …

What's your favourite animal at the museum?

I like the lions best.

My personal words

Body parts

Stand on one leg, please.

Can you hop to the board?

This is an elephant's leg.

My monster has got a red head.

My personal words

Sports and hobbies

Jobs

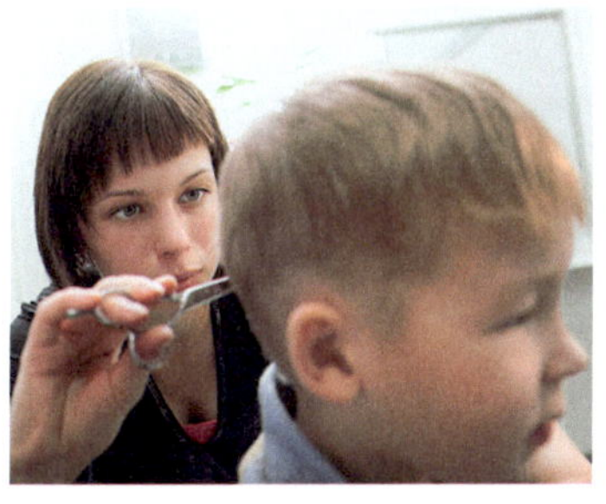

Sports and hobbies

Can you ride a horse?

No, I can't. What about you?

I can ride a horse.

How many children can ride a horse?

My personal words

Jobs

My brother's name is Matt.

What's his job?

He's a police officer.

What's your mum's job?

She's a teacher.

My personal words

Dear ____________,

Please come to our play:

____

When

On ____________

at ____________

Where

____

From,

____

A school play

1
Guy Fawkes
This book belongs to:
2
London, autumn 1605
Let's kill the king.
3
Yes, let's kill the king with gunpowder.
4
...33... 34...35...36. OK. Let's go.
5
Look at the gunpowder! It's a plot!
6
That's treason!
7
You won't kill the king!
8
Remember, remember
The fifth of November,
Gunpowder, treason and plot.
I see no reason
Why gunpowder treason
Should ever be forgot.

Classroom talk

What my teacher says:

Sit in a circle, please.

Go back to your chair, please.

Open the window, please.

Shut the door, please.

Put your hands up, please.

Clean the blackboard, please.

Let's play a game.

Let's sing a song.

What I say:

Du möchtest zur Toilette gehen. — Can I go to the toilet, please?

Du bist zu spät gekommen. — Sorry, I'm late.

Du hast deine Hausaufgaben vergessen. — Sorry, I forgot my homework.

Du bist mit deiner Aufgabe fertig. — I've finished.

Sunshine

Lehrwerk für den früh beginnenden Englischunterricht

Activity Book 4

Erarbeitet von
Stefanie Aschkar, Konstanz; Tanja Beattie, Ebersberg; Nadine Kerler, Ulm; Caroline Schröder, München; Maria Skejic, Frankfurt am Main

Auf der Grundlage der Ausgabe von
Birgit Hollbrügge, Bielefeld; Ulrike Kraaz, Werther

Beratende Mitwirkung
Uwe Becker, Mannheim; Margit Butscher-Wich, Bad Abbach; Michael Duscha, Braunschweig; Renate Hafner, Blaustein; Siân Williams-Hahn, Schorndorf (englischsprachige Texte)

Verlagsredaktion
Daniela Aue

Illustration
Beehive Illustration, Cirencester, England: Mike Phillips, Neil Chapman; Volker Fredrich, Hamburg; Mary Hall, Bath, England

Gesamtgestaltung
Corinna Babylon, Berlin

Technische Umsetzung
Michaela Müller für agentur corngreen, Leipzig

www.cornelsen.de

Alle Drucke dieser Auflage sind inhaltlich unverändert und können im Unterricht nebeneinander verwendet werden.

Druck: H. Heenemann, Berlin

1. Auflage, 7. Druck 2023
Activity Book mit Audio-CD
978-3-06-083767-0

1. Auflage, 1. Druck 2018
Activity Book mit Audio-CD und interaktiven Übungen
978-3-06-081539-5

PEFC zertifiziert
Dieses Produkt stammt aus nachhaltig bewirtschafteten Wäldern und kontrollierten Quellen.
www.pefc.de
PEFC/04-31-1156

Quellenangaben

Kapitelicons
Kalender: Mega Pixel/Shutterstock.com; Kind: Imago Stock & People GmbH/Westend61; Fußball: stock.adobe.com/Andrey Kiselev; Käse: stock.adobe.com/pink-coala; Bus: stock.adobe.com/Ludmila Smite; Wecker: stock.adobe.com/Cobalt; Ahorn: stock.adobe.com/Africa Studio; Elefant: pandapaw/Shutterstock.com; Füße: mauritius images/Photoshot Creative; Pfeil: xtock/Shutterstock.com; Familie: picture alliance/ASSOCIATED PRESS; Kamm und Schere: stock.adobe.com/odluap; Freiheitsstatue: stock.adobe.com/LittleSteven65; Keyboard: stock.adobe.com/momi-us; Maulwurf: Lox oderBergmann; Feuerwerk: Steve Allen/Shutterstock.com; Zweig: n_defender/Shutterstock.com; Kürbisfratze: stock.adobe.com/Pioppo.

Bilder
Seite 7: mauritius images/ian nolan/Alamy (Bild 01 + 04); stock.adobe.com/Maksim Shebeka (Bild 02); stock.adobe.com/Bondarau (Bild 03); mauritius images/Oleksiy Maksymenko/Alamy (Bild 05); mauritius images/John Bradshaw/Alamy (Bild 06); Seite 10 (v. l. n. r.): stock.adobe.com/chrisdorney; mauritius images/Loop Images; Cornelsen/Daniela Aue; stock.adobe.com/william87; mauritius images/Justin Kase zsixz/Alamy; Cornelsen/Daniela Aue; stock.adobe.com/kmiragaya; stock.adobe.com/Janis Smits; stock.adobe.com/sborisov; mauritius images/Alvey & Towers Picture Library/Alamy; mauritius images/Prisma; stock.adobe.com/philipus; Seite 32: stock.adobe.com/Stefan Yang; stock.adobe.com/Evgeny Skidanov; stock.adobe.com/Ad van Brunschot; stock.adobe.com/odluap; stock.adobe.com/Thomas Jansa; stock.adobe.com/Denis Nata; Seite 35: E-Mail-Fenster: stock.adobe.com/Maxim Grebeshkov; Seite 39: (v. o. n. u): Cornelsen/Daniela Aue; stock.adobe.com/kmiragaya; stock.adobe.com/chrisdorney; stock.adobe.com/Janis Smits; mauritius images/Loop Images; stock.adobe.com/sborisov; Seite 47: picture alliance/empics (Bild 01); picture alliance/REUTERS (Bild 2); Featureflash Photo Agency/Shutterstock.com (Bild 03); picture alliance/Photoshot (Bild 04); Shaun Jeffers/Shutterstock.com (Bild 05 + 06); Bild 7 zeigt Prince George bei der Taufe von Prinzessin Charlotte in Sandringham am 5. 7. 2015: picture alliance/REUTERS; Seite 48–50: Puppet Empire © 2015 Cornelsen Schulverlage GmbH; Seite 51: mauritius images/Roberto Herrett/Alamy; mauritius images/Jeff Greenberg/Alamy; mauritius images/Eric Farrelly/Alamy; mauritius images/Eric Farrelly/Alamy; mauritius images/Elena Chaykina/Alamy; mauritius images/Jeffrey Blackler/Alamy; mauritius images/Kevin George/Alamy; stock.adobe.com/philipus; stock.adobe.com/william87; mauritius images/Justin Kase zsixz/Alamy; Cornelsen/Daniela Aue; mauritius images/Alvey & Towers Picture Library/Alamy; mauritius images/Prisma; stock.adobe.com/Dmitriy Sladkov; Senohrabek/Shutterstock.com; Seite 53: stock.adobe.com/Elena Schweitzer; stock.adobe.com/A_Bruno; Nitr/Shutterstock.com; stock.adobe.com/Viktor; stock.adobe.com/sheva_ua; stock.adobe.com/PhotoSG; stock.adobe.com/Robert Hoetink; stock.adobe.com/chungking; stock.adobe.com/Gudellaphoto; Ellen McKnight/Shutterstock.com; stock.adobe.com/Bikeworldtravel; stock.adobe.com/Jürgen Fälchle; Seite 55: Audrey Snider-Bell/Shutterstock.com; reptiles4all/Shutterstock.com; Maggy Meyer/Shutterstock.com; MartinMaritz/Shutterstock.com; andamanec/Shutterstock.com; aaltair/Shutterstock.com; Michael Potter11/Shutterstock.com; Ethan Daniels/Shutterstock.com; stock.adobe.com/dimedrol68; stock.adobe.com/matka_Wariatka; stock.adobe.com/schankz; stock.adobe.com/Timo Blaschke; stock.adobe.com/AB Photography; stock.adobe.com/matka_Wariatka; Seite 57: stock.adobe.com/imageegami; stock.adobe.com/st-fotograf; stock.adobe.com/lunaundmo; stock.adobe.com/Pavla Zakova; stock.adobe.com/Artranq; stock.adobe.com/andreyfire; stock.adobe.com/Deyan Georgiev; stock.adobe.com/Firma V; mauritius images/Justin Kase zsixz/Alamy; stock.adobe.com/Christian Schwier; stock.adobe.com/Karin &Uwe Annas; stock.adobe.com/danr13; John Roman Images/Shutterstock.com; ArtWell/Shutterstock.com.

Minibildkarten
(v. l. n. r.): Days of the week: mauritius images/Roberto Herrett/Alamy; mauritius images/Jeff Greenberg/Alamy; mauritius images/Eric Farrelly/Alamy; mauritius images/Eric Farrelly/Alamy; mauritius images/Elena Chaykina/Alamy; mauritius images/Jeffrey Blackler/Alamy; mauritius images/Kevin George/Alamy; Transport: stock.adobe.com/philipus; stock.adobe.com/william87; mauritius images/Justin Kase zsixz/Alamy; stock.adobe.com/Dmitriy Sladkov; Cornelsen/Daniela Aue; Senohrabek/Shutterstock.com; mauritius images/Alvey & Towers Picture Library/Alamy; mauritius images/Prisma; London sights/Food: stock.adobe.com/Tony Baggett; mauritius images/Loop Images; stock.adobe.com/giemmephoto; stock.adobe.com/kmiragaya; mauritius images/United Archives/World History Archive; ClipDealer GmbH/Claudio Divizia; stock.adobe.com/stocksolutions; stock.adobe.com/Elena Schweitzer; stock.adobe.com/PhotoSG; ClipDealer GmbH/Givaga; Food/Weather: Nitr/Shutterstock.com; stock.adobe.com/A_Bruno; stock.adobe.com/sheva_ua; stock.adobe.com/Gudellaphoto; stock.adobe.com/Bikeworldtravel; stock.adobe.com/Jürgen Fälchle; Ellen McKnight/Shutterstock.com; stock.adobe.com/chungking; stock.adobe.com/Robert Hoetink; Animals: stock.adobe.com/Rhombur; Audrey Snider-Bell/Shutterstock.com; Michael Potter11/Shutterstock.com; MartinMaritz/Shutterstock.com; Maggy Meyer/Shutterstock.com; andamanec/Shutterstock.com; aaltair/Shutterstock.com; reptiles4all/Shutterstock.com; Ethan Daniels/Shutterstock.com; Body parts / Sports: ClipDealer GmbH/Sergii Figurni; stock.adobe.com/matka_Wariatka; stock.adobe.com/AB Photography; stock.adobe.com/dimedrol68; stock.adobe.com/Timo Blaschke; stock.adobe.com/tan4ikk; stock.adobe.com/underdogstudios; stock.adobe.com/schankz; stock.adobe.com/matka_Wariatka; stock.adobe.com/Artranq; stock.adobe.com/ andreyfire; Sports/ Jobs: stock.adobe.com/imageegami; stock.adobe.com/st-fotograf; stock.adobe.com/lunaundmo; stock.adobe.com/Pavla Zakova; stock.adobe.com/Firma V; stock.adobe.com/Deyan Georgiev; ClipDealer GmbH/Discovod; stock.adobe.com/Karin & Uwe Annas; John Roman Images/Shutterstock.com; ArtWell/Shutterstock.com; mauritius images/Justin Kase zsixz/Alamy; stock.adobe.com/Christian Schwier; Halloween / Bonfire: stock.adobe.com/Kzenon; ClipDealer GmbH/July Sun; stock.adobe.com/Pioppo; ClipDealer GmbH/Andrey Armyagov; ClipDealer GmbH/© www.isselee.de/© www.lifeonwhitre.eu; ClipDealer GmbH/Monkey Business Images; stock.adobe.com/iagodina; Cristian Gusa/Shutterstock.com; Steve Allen/Shutterstock.com; stock.adobe.com/Myrna Schwartinsky; mauritius images/FLPA/Alamy.

Texte
Seite 17 (u.) © Sheila Margaret Ward; Seite 46: RUDOLPH THE RED NOSED REINDEER, ST. NICHOLAS-MUSIC INC., WARNER CHAPPEL MUSIC UK, Chappell & Co. GmbH & Co. KG, Hamburg/Johnny Marks (Text)

Days of the week

Monday
Tuesday
Wednesday
Thursday
Friday
Saturday
Sunday

Transport

boat
bus
car
motorbike
plane
taxi
train
underground

London sights

Big Ben
Buckingham Palace
the London Eye
London Zoo
the River Thames
Tower Bridge

Food

butter
cheese
chicken
chips
egg
ham
salad

Weather

cloudy
foggy
rainy
snowy
sunny
windy

Animals

camel
crocodile
elephant
hippo
lion
monkey
parrot
snake
whale

Body parts

arm
back
foot
head
knee
leg
shoulder
toe
tummy

Sports

do ballet
do judo
play basketball
play table tennis
ride a horse
ski
snowboard
swim

Jobs

hairdresser
mechanic
police officer
shop assistant
taxi driver
teacher

Halloween

ghost
monster
pumpkin
skeleton
spider
vampire
witch

Bonfire Night

bonfire
fireworks
Guy Fawkes
king